Name

Draw a Picture

I Can...

- [ ] use a Capital Letter
  <u>T</u>he cat is big.
- [ ] use spaces
- [ ] sound out words
  d-o-g = dog
- [ ] use a Period .
- [ ] Draw a picture

He is having fun, running under the sun with his new toy gun.

fun	gun	run	sun
vui vẻ	súng	chạy	mặt trời

Name: ______________________ Date: ______________________

Today is: Monday | Tuesday | Wednesday | Thursday | Friday

Direction: Trace and read the sentences.

bag	rag	tag	wag

túi	giẻ	nhãn	vẫy

He has many bags.

I see a rag.

I see a tag.

Its tail is wagging.

My Sight Word List

a	in	said
and	is	see
away	it	the
big	jump	three
blue	little	to
can	look	two
come	make	up
down	me	we
find	my	where
for	not	yellow
funny	one	you
go	day	
help	play	
here	red	
I	run	

Name: ____________________ Date: ____________________

Today is: Monday | Tuesday | Wednesday | Thursday | Friday

Direction: Trace and read the sentences.

fun	gun	run	sun
	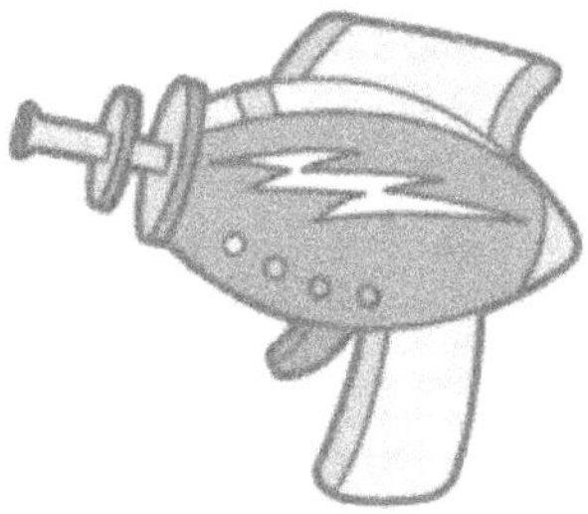		
vui vẻ	súng	chạy	mặt trời

They are having fun.

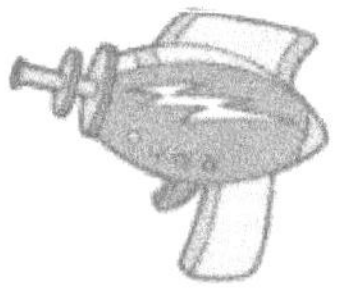

He has a gun.

The bear is running.

The sun is smiling.

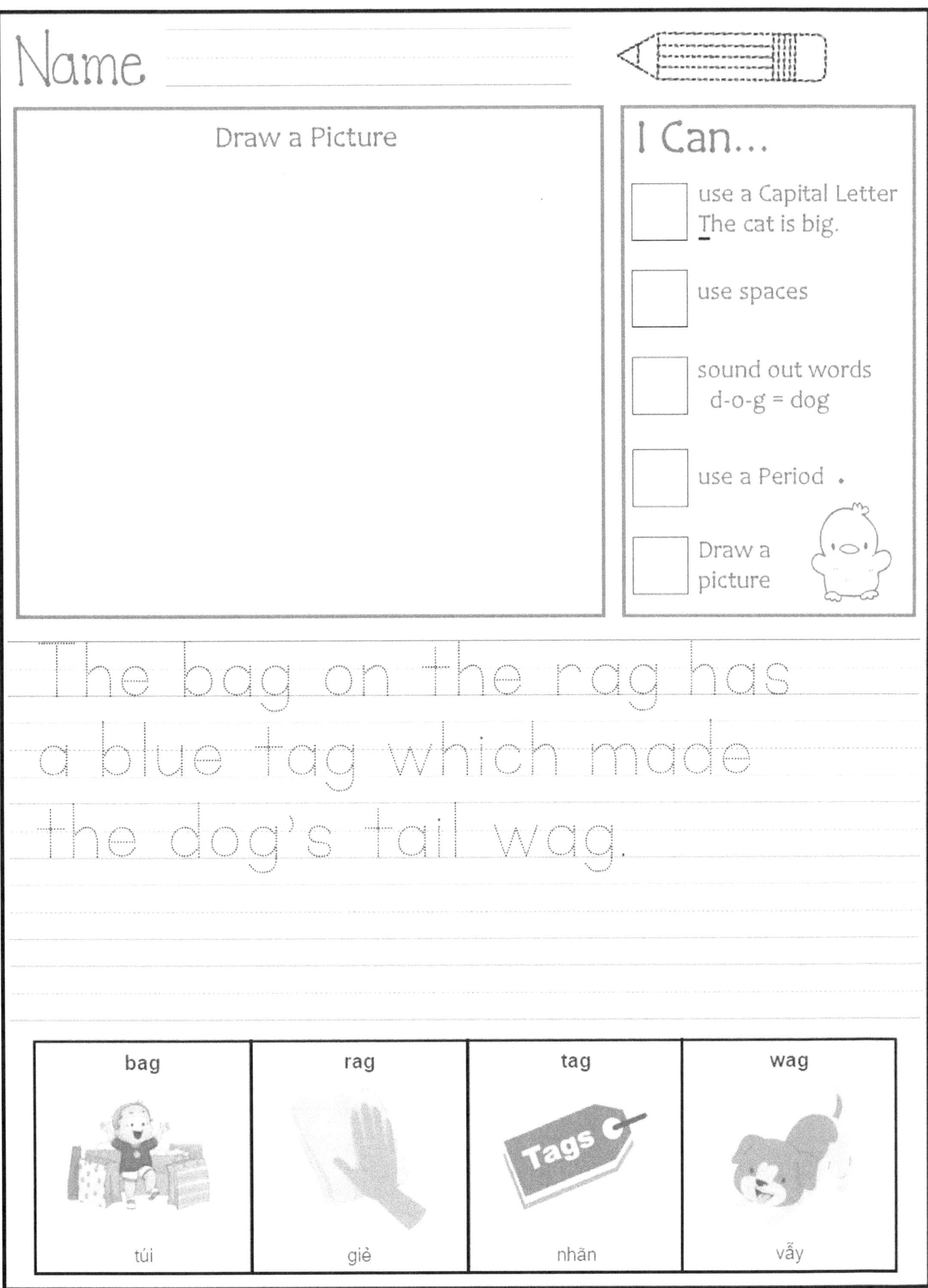

Name

Draw a Picture

I Can...

- [ ] use a Capital Letter
  <u>T</u>he cat is big.
- [ ] use spaces
- [ ] sound out words
  d-o-g = dog
- [ ] use a Period .
- [ ] Draw a picture

The bag on the rag has
a blue tag which made
the dog's tail wag.

bag	rag	tag	wag
túi	giẻ	nhãn	vẫy

Name: _______________ Date: _______________

Today is: Monday | Tuesday | Wednesday
Thursday | Friday

Direction: Trace and read the sentences.

can	man	pan	van
một lon	đàn ông	chảo	xe tải

I see a can of soda.

The man is happy.

The pan is dirty.

I see a big van.

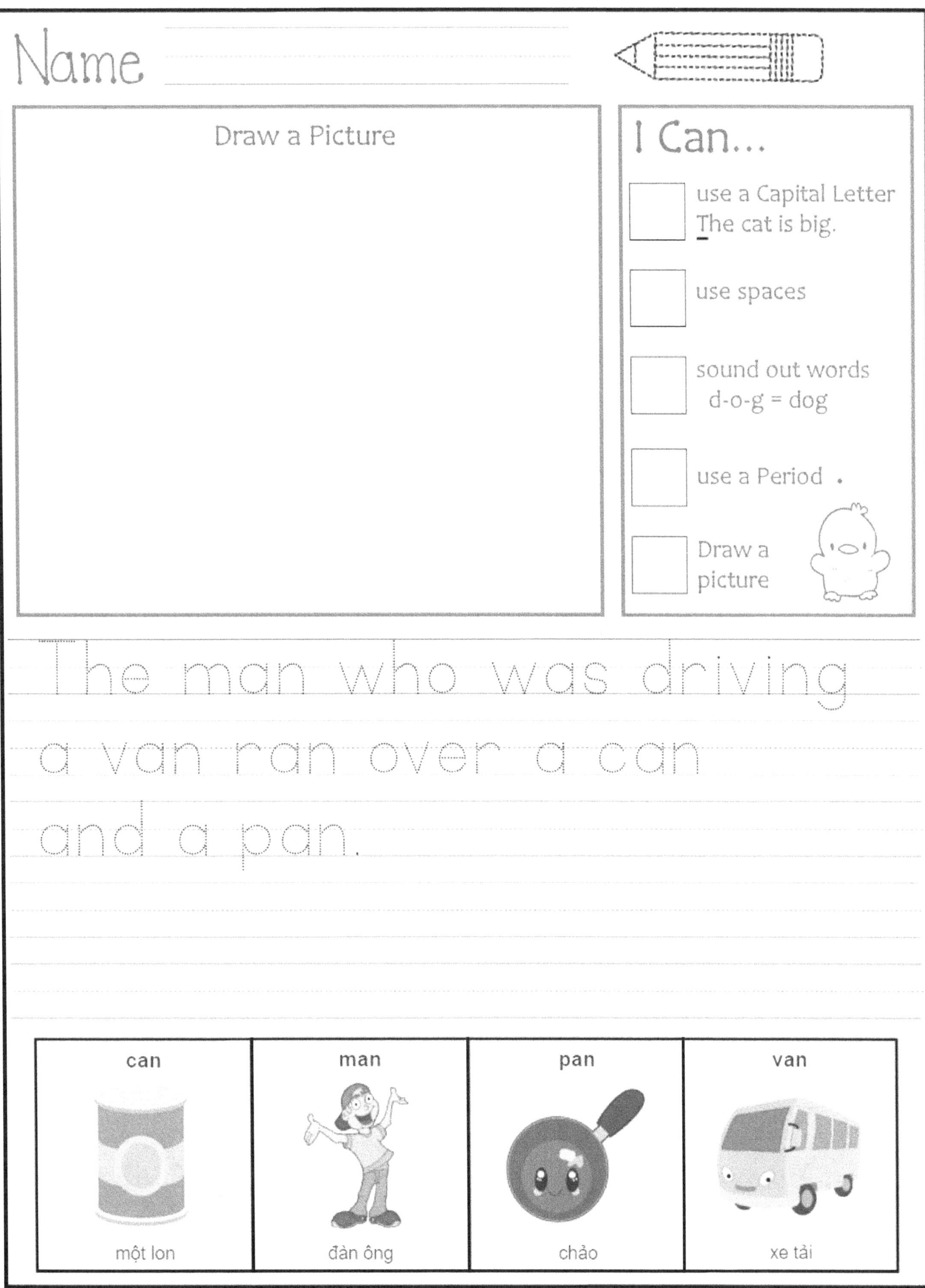

Name
Draw a Picture
I Can...
use a Capital Letter
The cat is big.
use spaces
sound out words
d-o-g = dog
use a Period .
Draw a picture
The man who was driving a van ran over a can and a pan.
can
một lon
man
đàn ông
pan
chảo
van
xe tải

Name: ____________________ Date: ____________________

Today is: Monday | Tuesday | Wednesday | Thursday | Friday

Direction: Trace and read the sentences.

cut	**gut**	**hut**	**nut**

cắt	ruột	túp lều	hạt

He cut his nails.

He has a gut.

This is a small hut.

It is holding a nut.

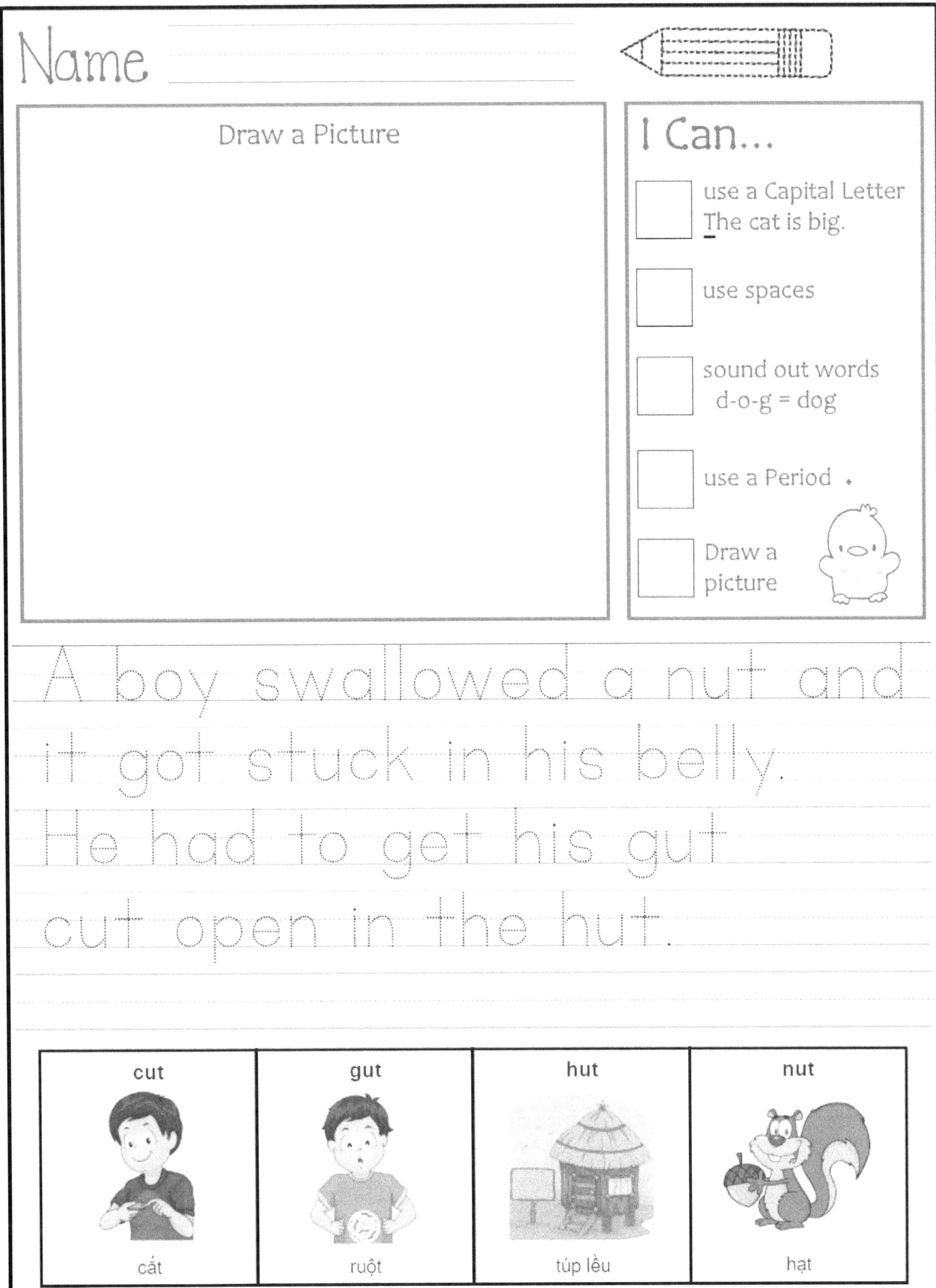

Name

Draw a Picture

I Can...

use a Capital Letter
The cat is big.

use spaces

sound out words
d-o-g = dog

use a Period .

Draw a
picture

A boy swallowed a nut and
it got stuck in his belly.
He had to get his gut
cut open in the hut.

cut

gut

hut

nut

cắt

ruột

túp lều

hạt

Direction: Trace and read the sentences.

fat	cat	hat	mat
mập	con mèo	mũ	chiếu

I see a fat dog.

This is my little cat.

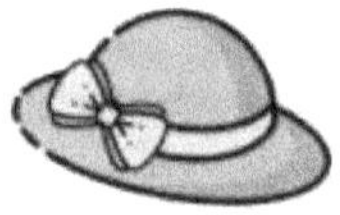

I like this hat.

I see a big mat.

Draw a Picture

I Can...

☐ use a Capital Letter
The cat is big.

☐ use spaces

☐ sound out words
d-o-g = dog

☐ use a Period .

☐ Draw a picture

The fat cat laid on the mat that was a hat pattern.

fat	cat	hat	mat
mập	con mèo	mũ	chiếu

Name: _______________ Date: _______________

Today is: Monday Tuesday Wednesday

Thursday Friday

Direction: Trace and read the sentences.

cab	lab	tab	crab
taxi	phòng thí nghiệm	chuyển hướng	cua

The cab is fast.

The lab is exciting.

The tab is long.

We found a crab.

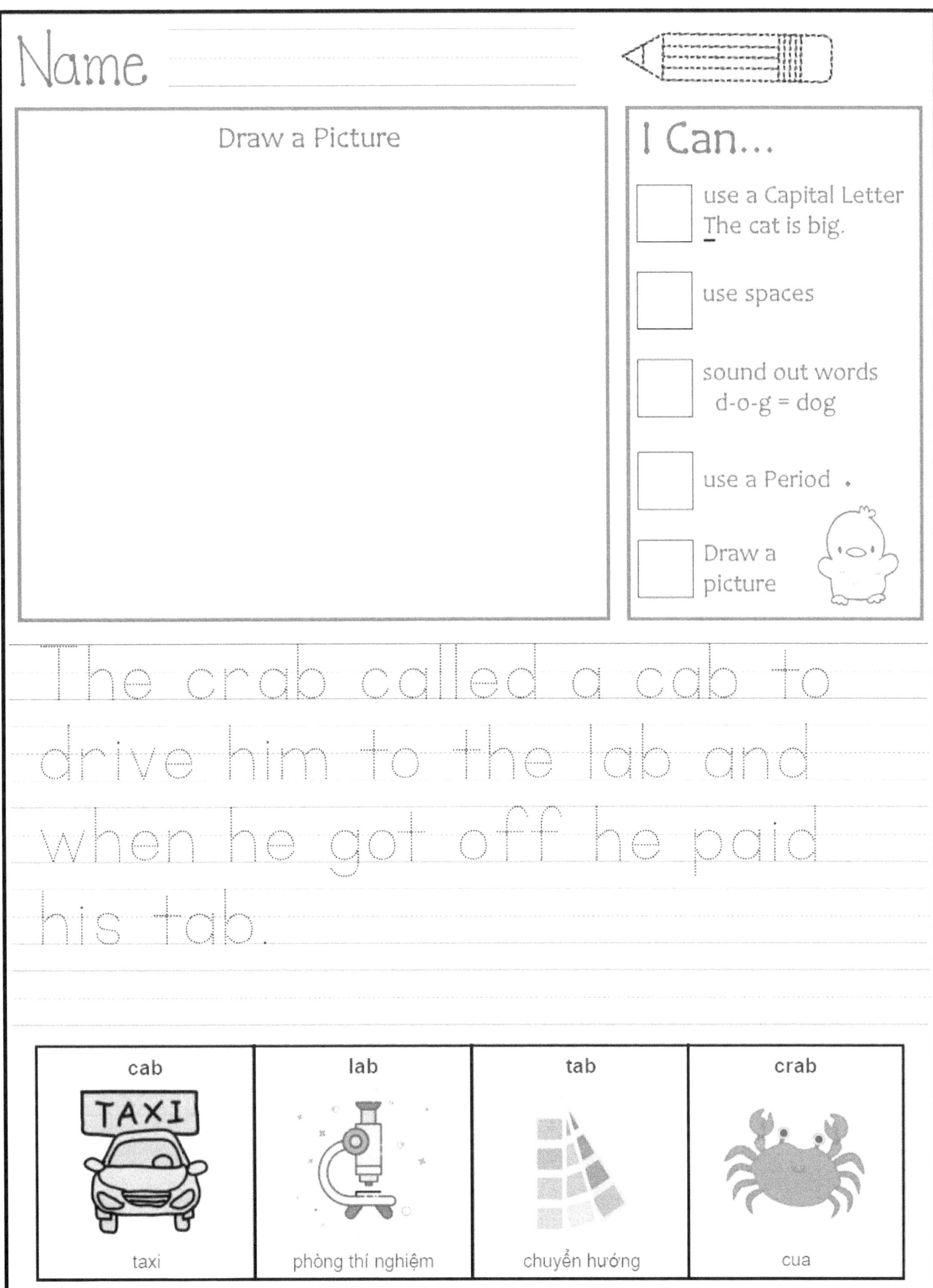

Name

Draw a Picture

I Can...

use a Capital Letter
The cat is big.

use spaces

sound out words
d-o-g = dog

use a Period .

Draw a
picture

The crab called a cab to drive him to the lab and when he got off he paid his tab.

cab
TAXI
taxi

lab
phòng thí nghiệm

tab
chuyển hướng

crab
cua

Name: ___________________ Date: ___________

Today is: Monday Tuesday Wednesday Thursday Friday

Direction: Trace and read the sentences.

ham	jam	ram	clam
giăm bông	mứt	cừu	vỏ

I like to eat ham.

We like to eat jam.

The ram is big.

The clam is pretty.

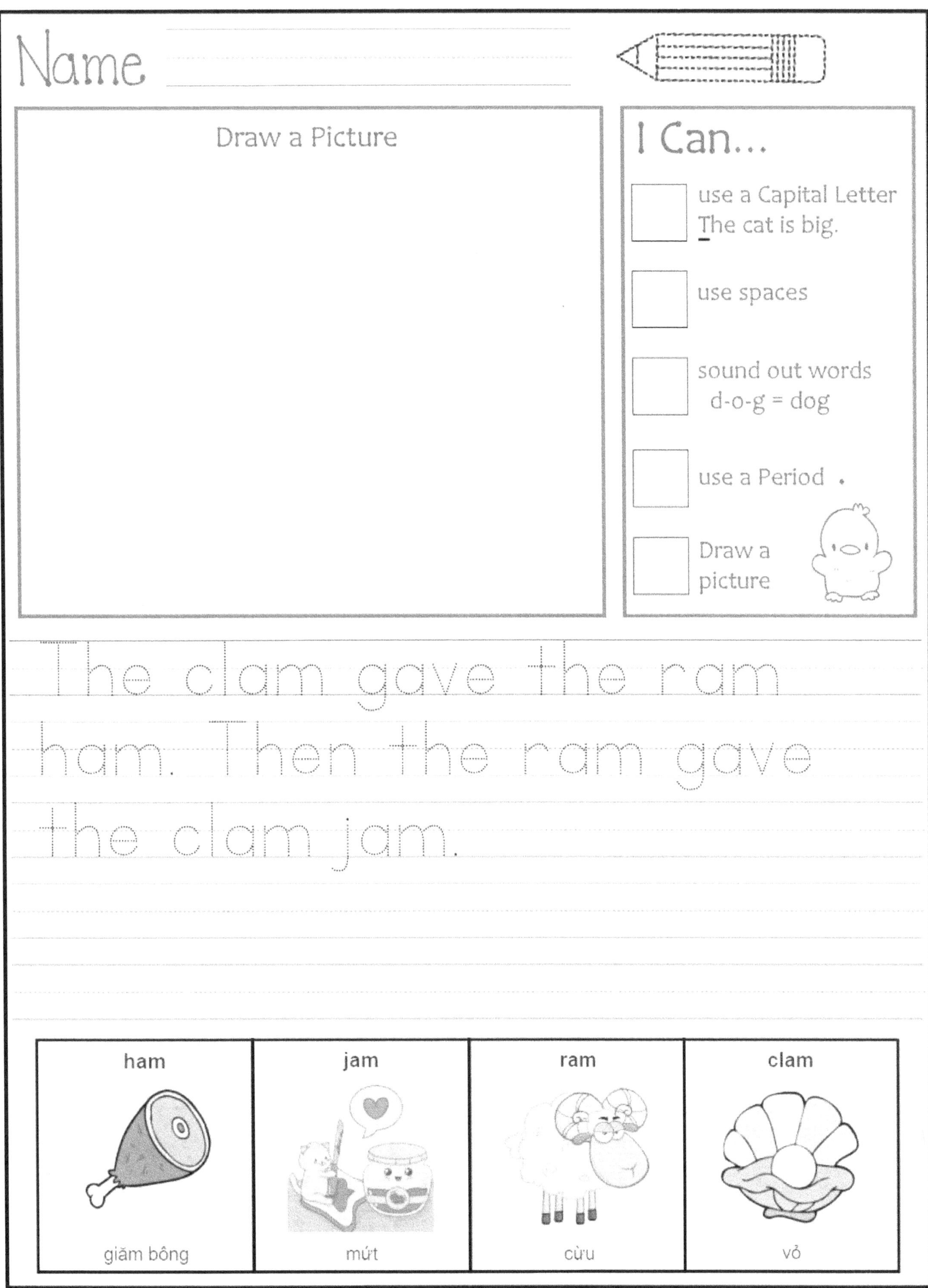

Name ___________

Draw a Picture

I Can...

- ☐ use a Capital Letter
  <u>T</u>he cat is big.
- ☐ use spaces
- ☐ sound out words
  d-o-g = dog
- ☐ use a Period .
- ☐ Draw a picture

The clam gave the ram ham. Then the ram gave the clam jam.

ham	jam	ram	clam
giăm bông	mứt	cừu	vỏ

Name: _______________________ Date: _______________

Today is: Monday Tuesday Wednesday
Thursday Friday

Direction: Trace and read the sentences.

bed	led	red	wed
giường	hàng đầu	màu đỏ	lễ cưới

This is my little bed.

He led us to safety.

The apple is red.

He asks her to wed.

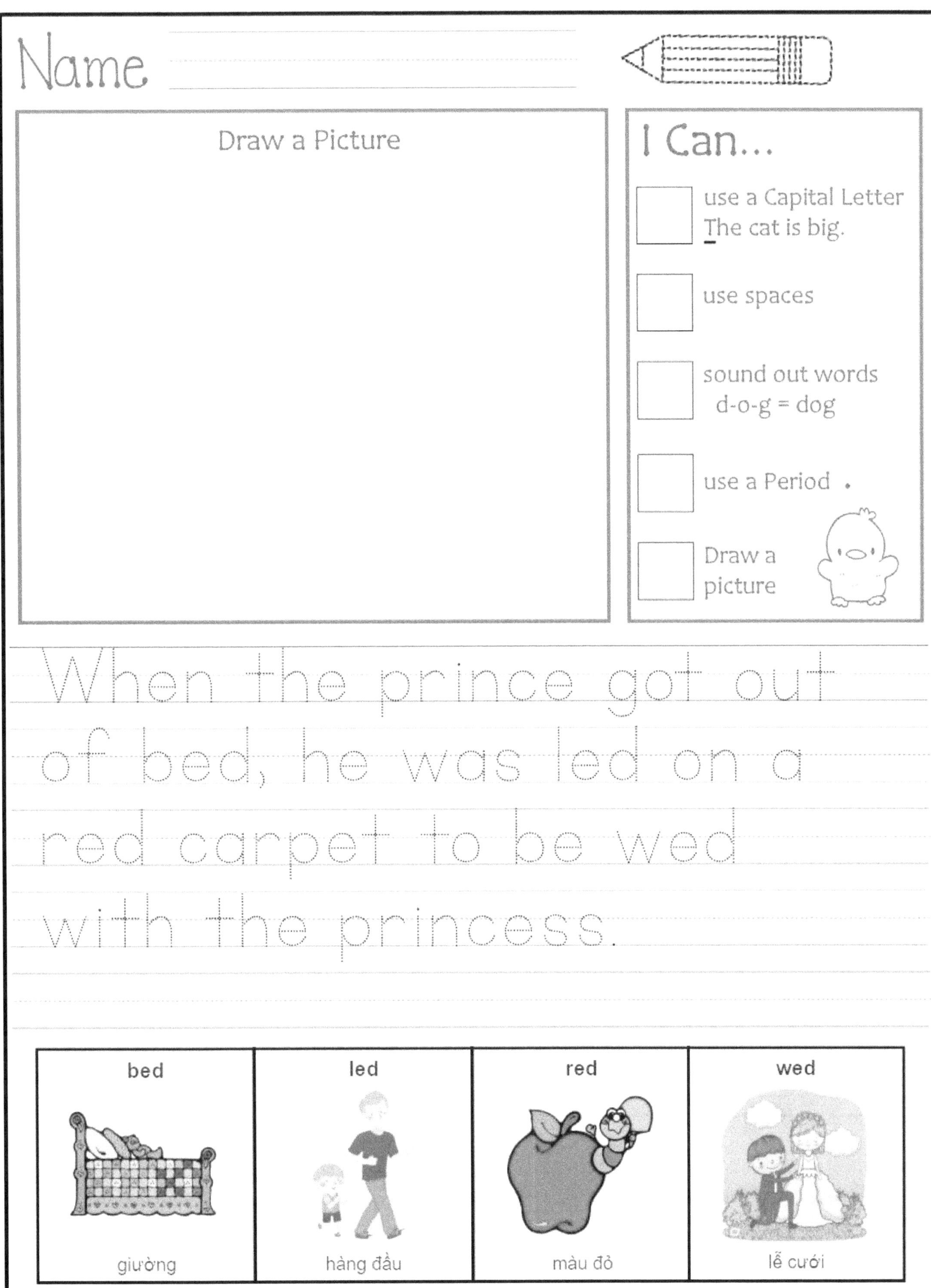

Name

Draw a Picture

I Can...

- [ ] use a Capital Letter
  <u>T</u>he cat is big.
- [ ] use spaces
- [ ] sound out words
  d-o-g = dog
- [ ] use a Period .
- [ ] Draw a picture

When the prince got out of bed, he was led on a red carpet to be wed with the princess.

bed	led	red	wed
giường	hàng đầu	màu đỏ	lễ cưới

Name: _________________ Date: _______________

Today is: | Monday | Tuesday | Wednesday |
| Thursday | Friday |

Direction: Trace and read the sentences.

| **bad** | **dad** | **mad** | **sad** |
| xấu | cha | điên | buồn |

This apple is bad.

My dad is very kind.

The reindeer is mad.

The little cat is sad.

Name

Draw a Picture

I Can...

☐ use a Capital Letter
The cat is big.

☐ use spaces

☐ sound out words
d-o-g = dog

☐ use a Period .

☐ Draw a picture

I was bad so my dad got mad and now I am so sad.

bad	dad	mad	sad
xấu	cha	điên	buồn

Name: __________________ Date: __________

Today is: [Monday] [Tuesday] [Wednesday]
[Thursday] [Friday]

Direction: Trace and read the sentences.

den	hen	pen	ten
từ chối	gà mái	chuồng ngựa	mười

It is a den.

The hens lay eggs.

She has a good pen.

The ten is smiling.

Draw a Picture

I Can...

- [ ] use a Capital Letter
  <u>T</u>he cat is big.
- [ ] use spaces
- [ ] sound out words
  d-o-g = dog
- [ ] use a Period .
- [ ] Draw a picture

The hen that lived in the
pen laid ten eggs
in her den.

den	hen	pen	ten
từ chối	gà mái	chuồng ngựa	mười

Name: _________________ Date: _________

Today is: Monday   Tuesday   Wednesday   Thursday   Friday

Direction: Trace and read the sentences.

gum	mum	sum	drum
kẹo dẻo	mẹ	tổng	trống

I like to chew gum.

My mum is kind!

I can do a sum!

The drum is big.

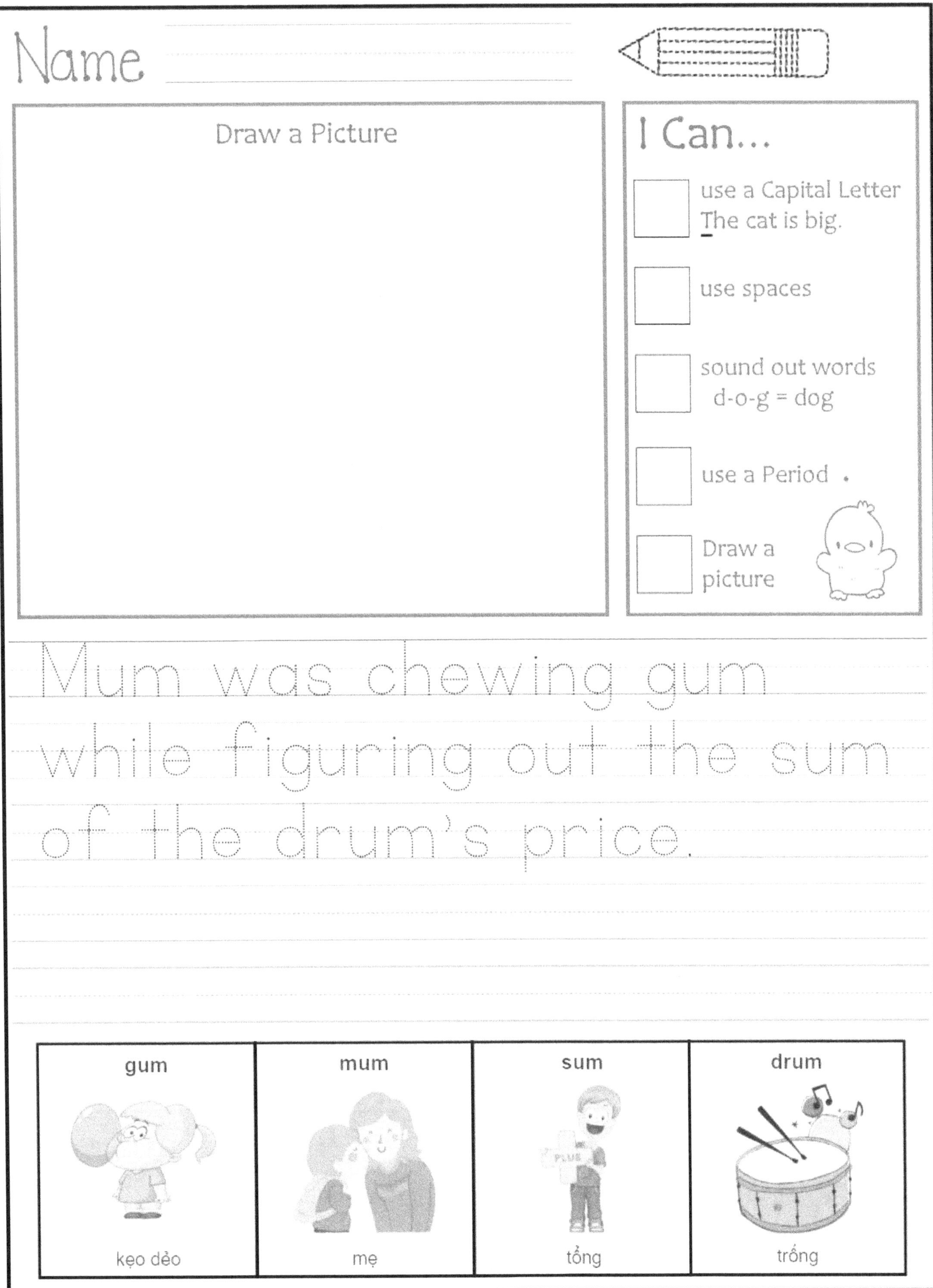

Name

Draw a Picture

I Can...

use a Capital Letter
The cat is big.

use spaces

sound out words
d-o-g = dog

use a Period .

Draw a
picture

Mum was chewing gum while figuring out the sum of the drum's price.

gum
kẹo dẻo

mum
mẹ

sum
tổng

drum
trống

Name: ______________________ Date: ______________________

Today is: Monday Tuesday Wednesday Thursday Friday

Direction: Trace and read the sentences.

bid	hid	kid	lid
			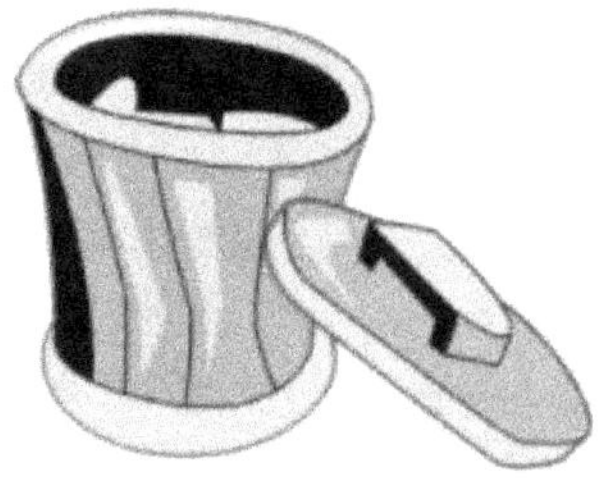
đấu thầu	ẩn giấu	đứa trẻ	nắp

He likes to bid.

He is hiding.

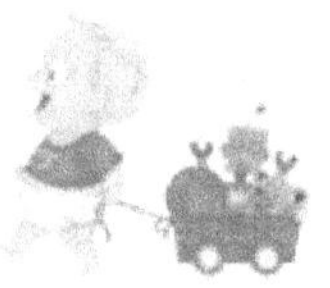

The kid like to play.

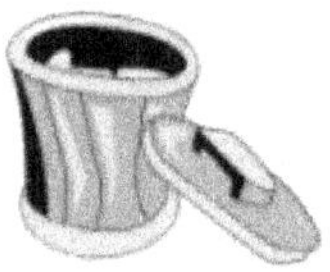

I see a lid.

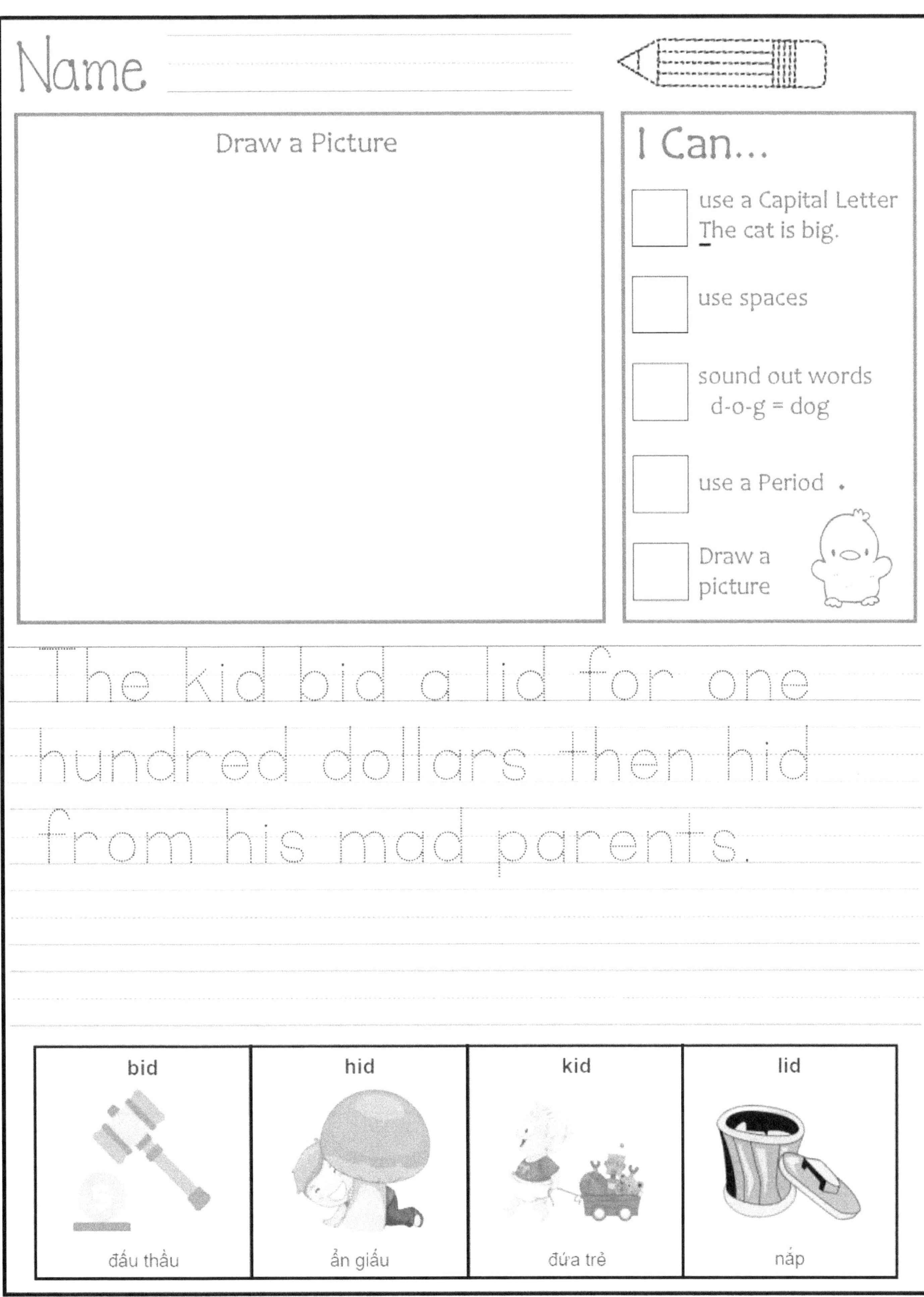

Name
Draw a Picture
I Can...
use a Capital Letter
The cat is big.
use spaces
sound out words
d-o-g = dog
use a Period .
Draw a picture
The kid bid a lid for one hundred dollars then hid from his mad parents.
bid
đấu thầu
hid
ẩn giấu
kid
đứa trẻ
lid
nắp

Name: ______________________ Date: ______________________

Today is: Monday | Tuesday | Wednesday | Thursday | Friday

Direction: Trace and read the sentences.

big	dig	pig	wig
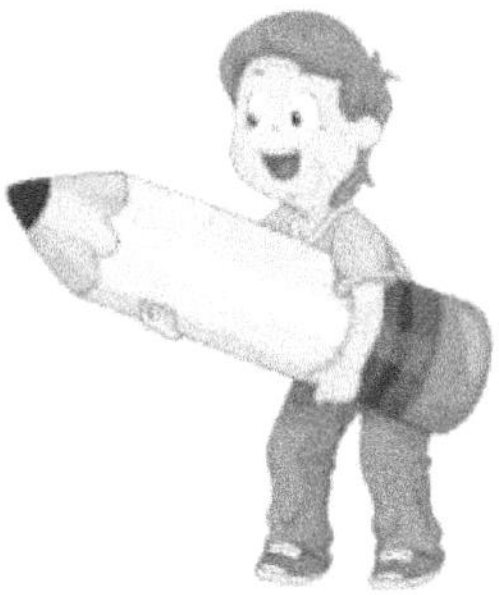	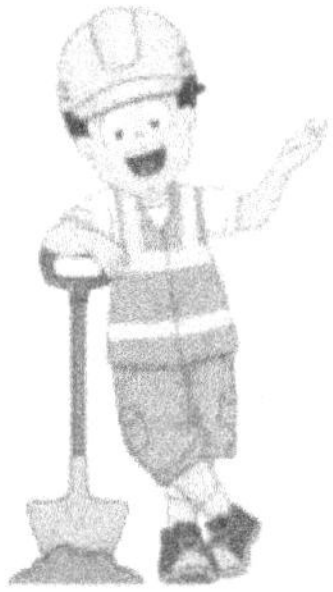	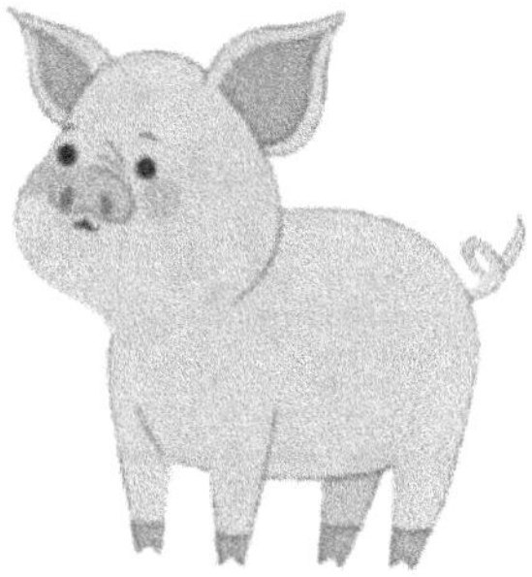	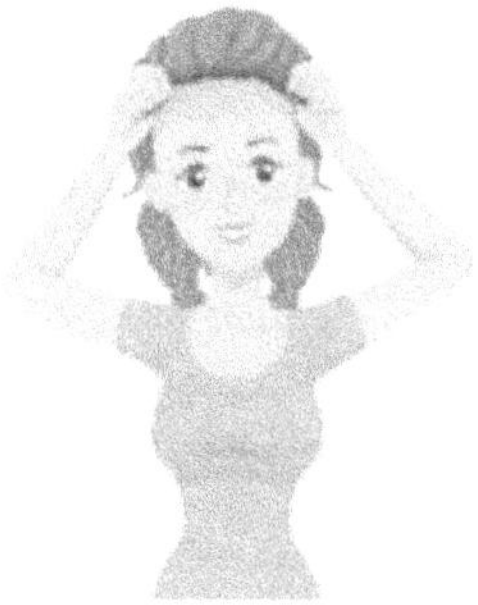
lớn	đào	con lợn	tóc giả

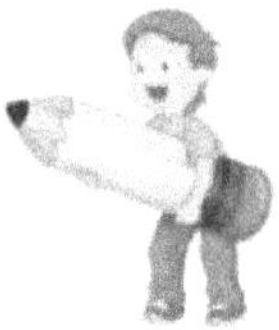

That is a big pencil.

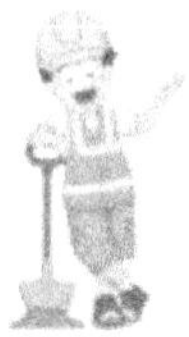

He will dig up a hole.

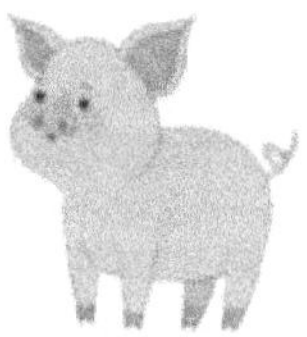

The pig is fat.

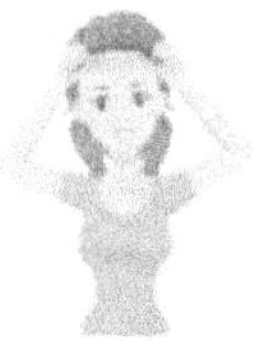

She puts on a wig.

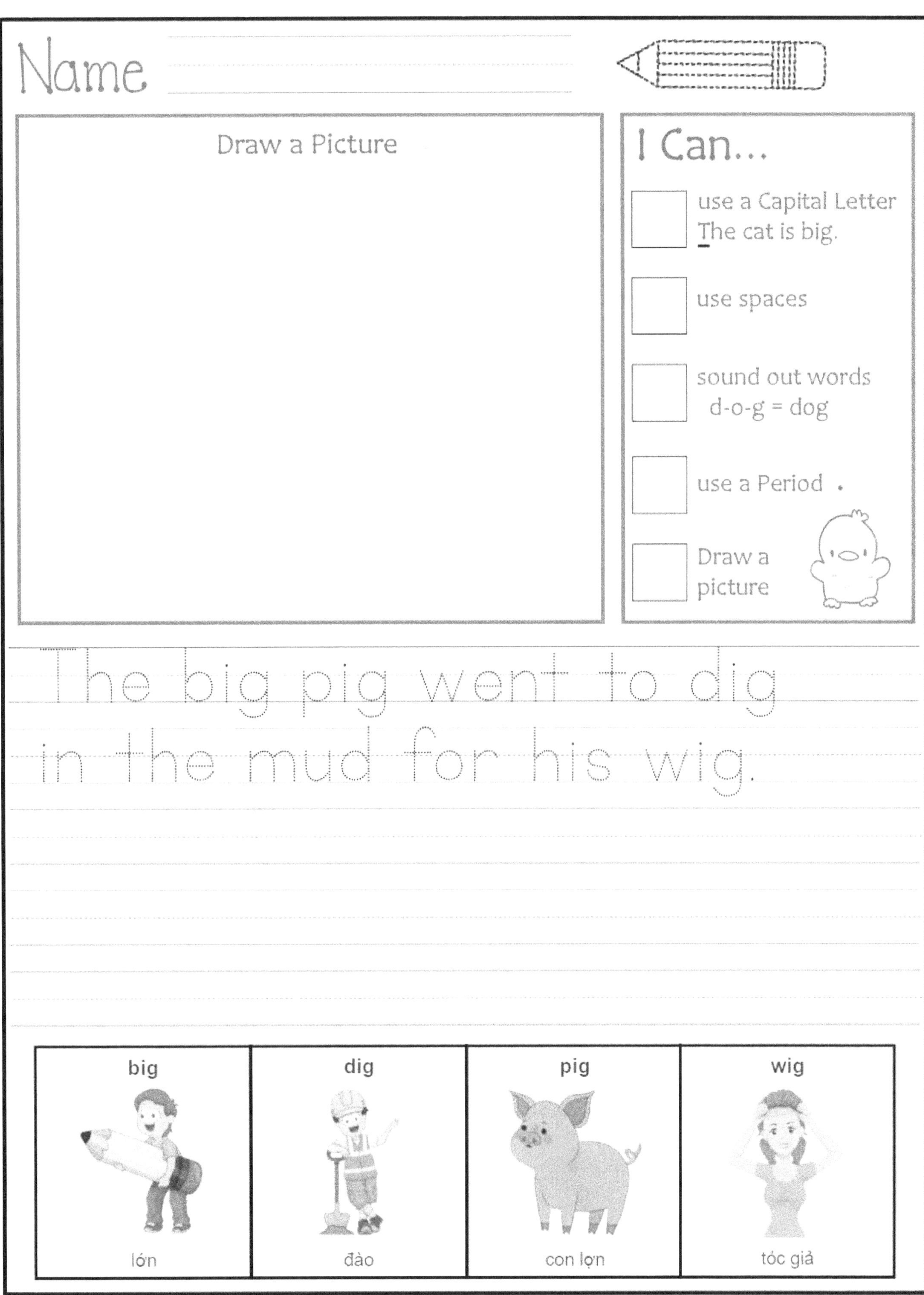

Name

Draw a Picture

I Can...
☐ use a Capital Letter
The cat is big.

☐ use spaces

☐ sound out words
d-o-g = dog

☐ use a Period .

☐ Draw a picture

The big pig went to dig in the mud for his wig.

big
lớn

dig
đào

pig
con lợn

wig
tóc giả

Name: ____________________ Date: ____________________

Today is: Monday | Tuesday | Wednesday | Thursday | Friday

Direction: Trace and read the sentences.

bin	fin	pin	win
	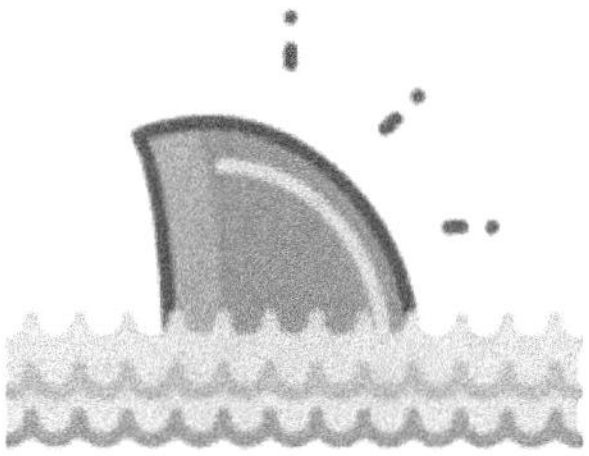		
một cái thùng	vây	ghim	thắng lợi

It is a recycle bin.

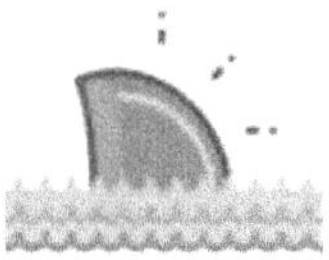

The shark has a fin.

The pin is pointy.

He won the match.

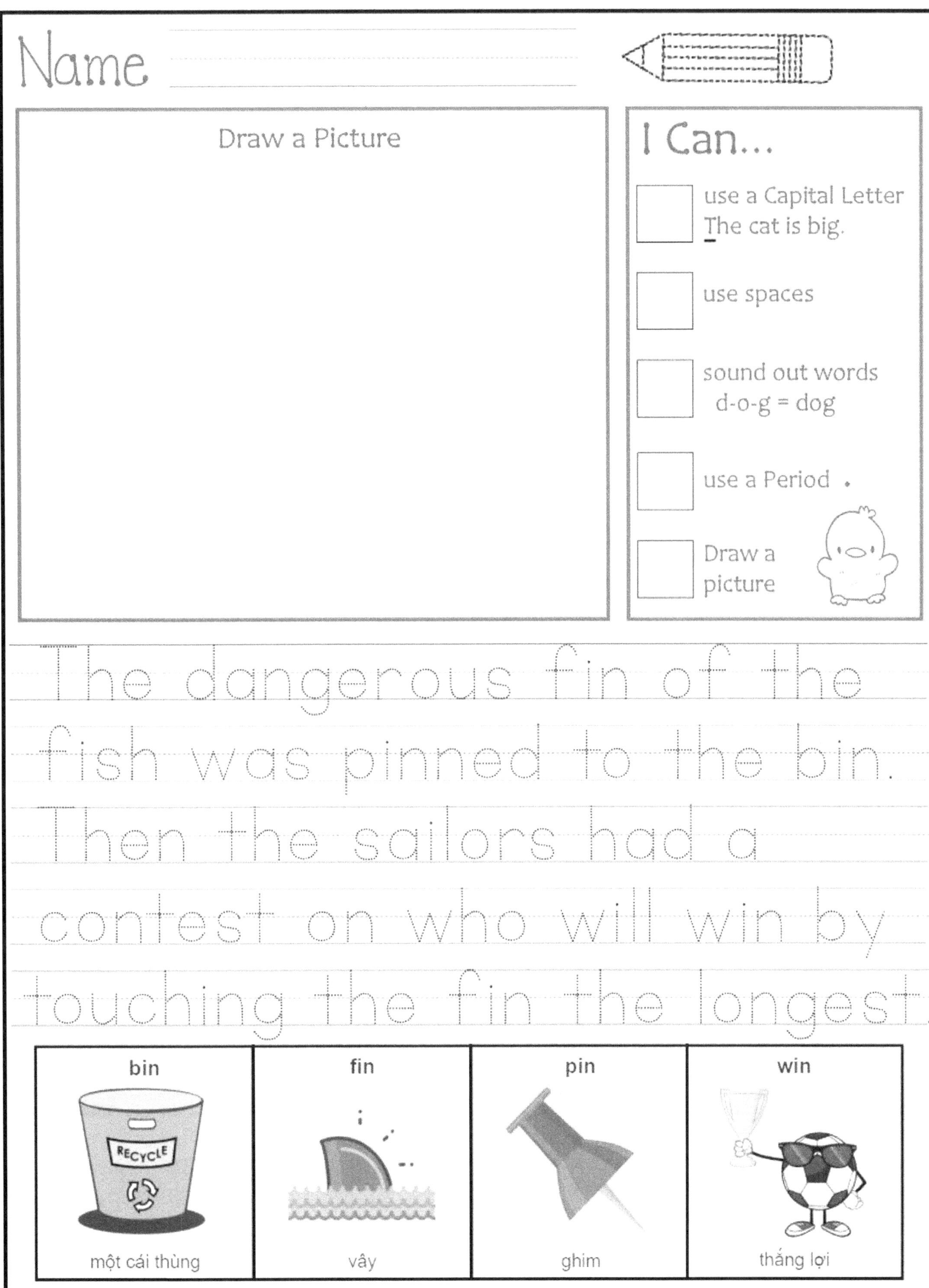

Name

Draw a Picture

I Can...
use a Capital Letter
The cat is big.

use spaces

sound out words
d-o-g = dog

use a Period .

Draw a
picture

The dangerous fin of the fish was pinned to the bin. Then the sailors had a contest on who will win by touching the fin the longest.

bin
RECYCLE
một cái thùng

fin
vây

pin
ghim

win
thắng lợi

Name: ______________________ Date: ______________________

Today is: Monday | Tuesday | Wednesday | Thursday | Friday

Direction: Trace and read the sentences.

hip	lip	nip	sip

hông	đôi môi	núm vú	uống

This is my hip.

Her lips are red.

It is nipping its toy.

She is sipping.

Name

Draw a Picture

I Can...

- [ ] use a Capital Letter
  <u>T</u>he cat is big.

- [ ] use spaces

- [ ] sound out words
  d-o-g = dog

- [ ] use a Period .

- [ ] Draw a
  picture

The dog nipped someone
who was sipping water
with his lip.

hip	lip	nip	sip
hông	đôi môi	núm vú	uống

Name: _______________________ Date: _______________

Today is: | Monday | Tuesday | Wednesday |
| Thursday | Friday |

Direction: Trace and read the sentences.

fit	**hit**	**kit**	**sit**
phù hợp	đánh	bộ dụng cụ	ngồi

It is perfectly fit.

They hit each other.

That is a safety kit.

He is sitting.

Draw a Picture

I Can...

- [ ] use a Capital Letter
  <u>T</u>he cat is big.

- [ ] use spaces

- [ ] sound out words
  d-o-g = dog

- [ ] use a Period .

- [ ] Draw a picture

The fit doctor sat then was hit by a kit.

fit	hit	kit	sit
phù hợp	đánh	bộ dụng cụ	ngồi

Name: ______________________ Date: ______________________

Today is: Monday Tuesday Wednesday Thursday Friday

Direction: Trace and read the sentences.

cob	job	rob	sob

ngô	việc làm	lấy trộm	khóc

 I ate corn on the cob.

 This is my job.

 He is robbing.

 The girl is sobbing.

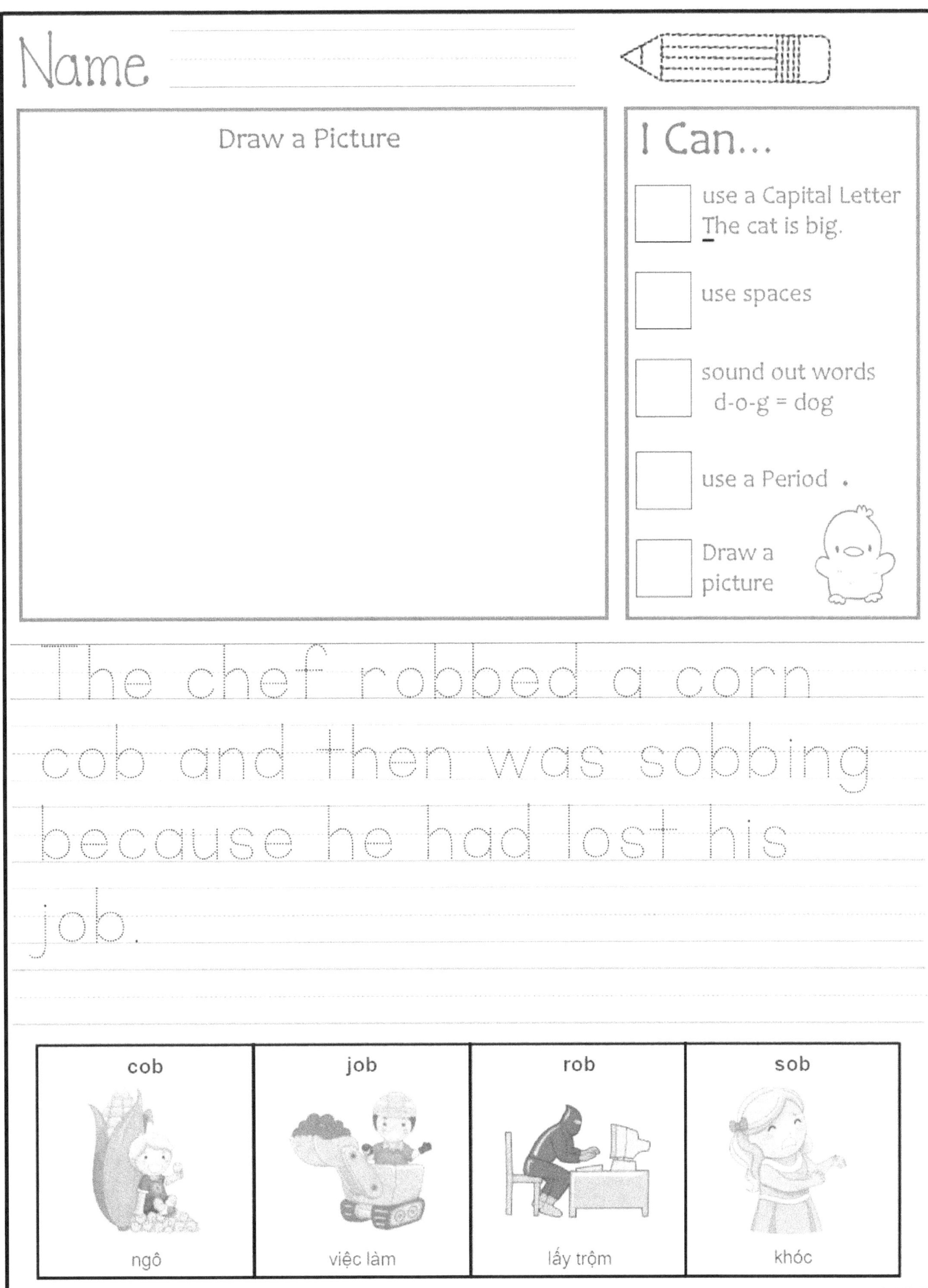

Name

Draw a Picture

I Can...

- [ ] use a Capital Letter
  <u>T</u>he cat is big.
- [ ] use spaces
- [ ] sound out words
  d-o-g = dog
- [ ] use a Period .
- [ ] Draw a picture

The chef robbed a corn cob and then was sobbing because he had lost his job.

cob	job	rob	sob
ngô	việc làm	lấy trộm	khóc

Name: ___________________ Date: __________

Today is: [Monday] [Tuesday] [Wednesday]
[Thursday] [Friday]

Direction: Trace and read the sentences.

dog	hog	jog	log
chó	lấy quá phần	chạy bộ	gỗ

The dog is thrilled.

The hog is big.

She is jogging.

The log is small.

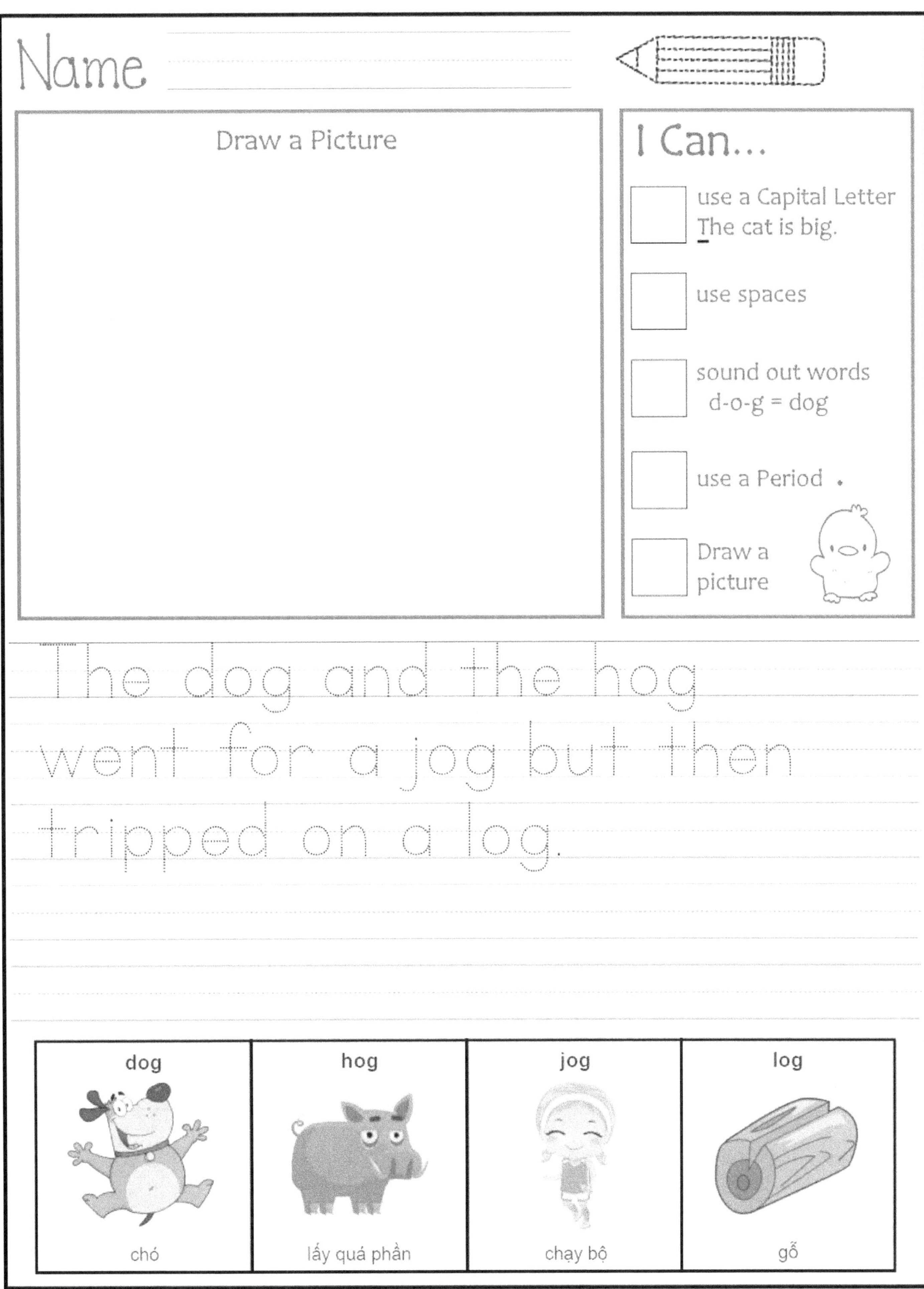

Name

Draw a Picture

I Can...

use a Capital Letter
The cat is big.

use spaces

sound out words
d-o-g = dog

use a Period .

Draw a
picture

The dog and the hog
went for a jog but then
tripped on a log.

dog
chó

hog
lấy quá phần

jog
chạy bộ

log
gỗ

Name: ____________________ Date: ____________________

Today is: Monday | Tuesday | Wednesday | Thursday | Friday

Direction: Trace and read the sentences.

bug	hug	jug	mug
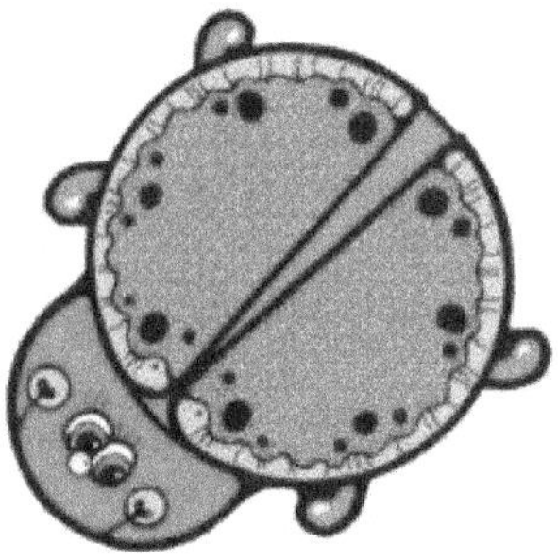			
bọ cánh cứng	ôm	cái bình	cái ca

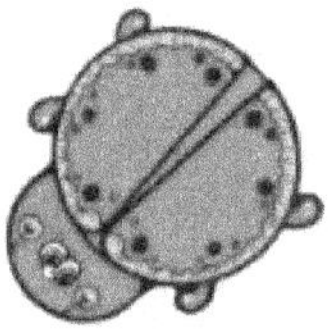
The bug is colorful.

She is hugging.

The jug has milk in it.

He has a mug.

Name
Draw a Picture
I Can...
use a Capital Letter
The cat is big.
use spaces
sound out words
d-o-g = dog
use a Period .
Draw a picture
The bug hugged the jug and the mug which was full of jam.
bug
hug
jug
mug
bọ cánh cứng
ôm
cái bình
cái ca

Name: _______________________ Date: _______________

Today is: | Monday | Tuesday | Wednesday |
| Thursday | Friday |

Direction: Trace and read the sentences.

| **cot** | **dot** | **hot** | **pot** |
| giường | dấu chấm | nóng bức | nồi |

This is my cot.

There are many dots.

It is very hot.

He has a plant pot.

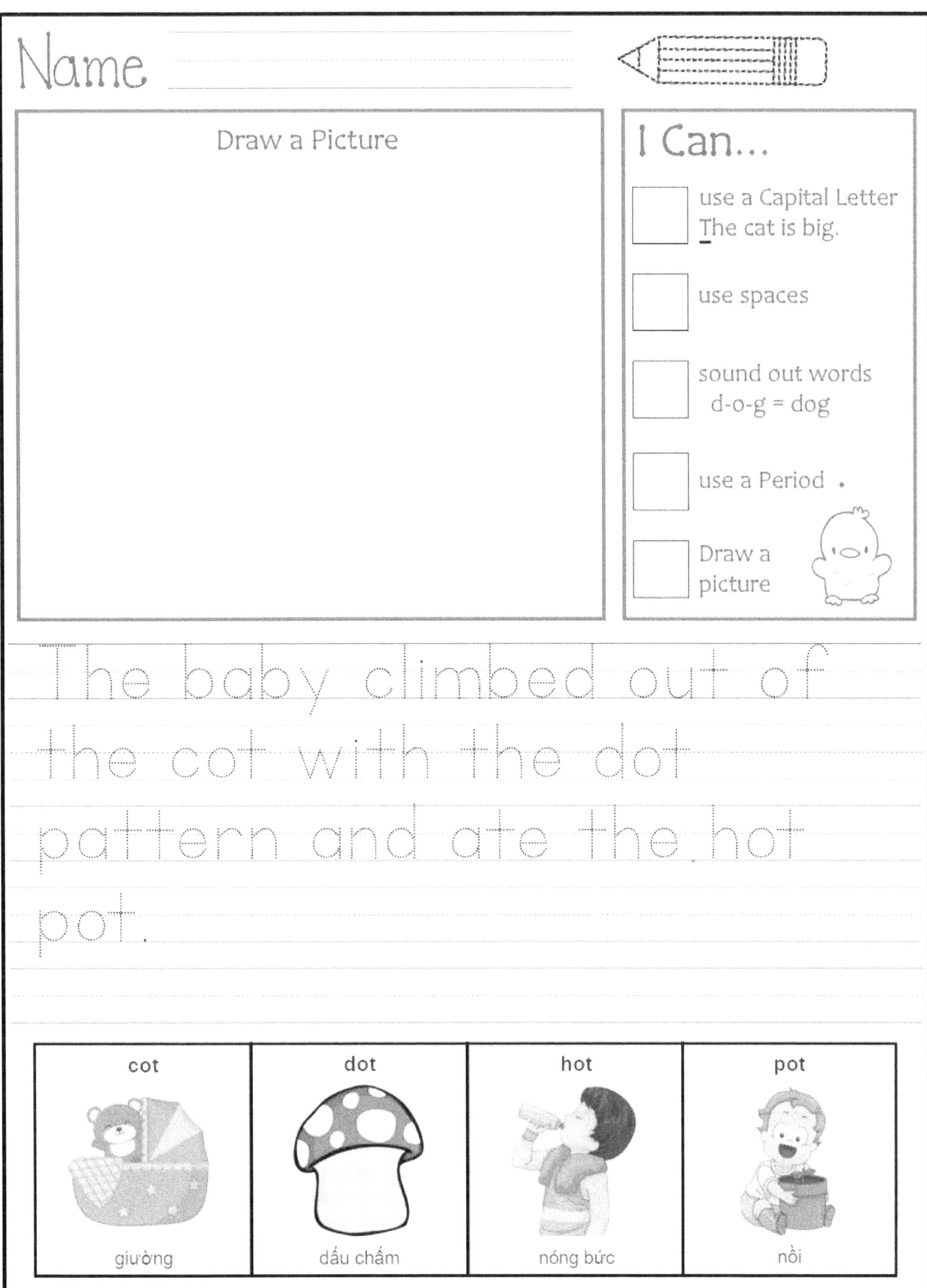

Name

Draw a Picture

I Can...

use a Capital Letter
The cat is big.

use spaces

sound out words
d-o-g = dog

use a Period .

Draw a
picture

The baby climbed out of
the cot with the dot
pattern and ate the hot
pot.

cot
giường

dot
dấu chấm

hot
nóng bức

pot
nồi

Name: _______________________ Date: _______________

Today is: [Monday] [Tuesday] [Wednesday]
[Thursday] [Friday]

Direction: Read the words and make a sentence.

fun	gun	run	sun
vui vẻ	súng	chạy	mặt trời

____

____

____

____

Name

Draw a Picture

I Can...

☐ use a Capital Letter
The cat is big.

☐ use spaces

☐ sound out words
d-o-g = dog

☐ use a Period .

☐ Draw a
picture

Name: _______________________   Date: _______________

Today is: Monday Tuesday Wednesday Thursday Friday

Name: _________________________ Date: _________________

Today is: [Monday] [Tuesday] [Wednesday]
[Thursday] [Friday]

Direction: Read the words and make a sentence.

bag	**rag**	**tag**	**wag**
túi	giẻ	nhãn	vẫy

Name

Draw a Picture

I Can...

- [ ] use a Capital Letter
  The cat is big.

- [ ] use spaces

- [ ] sound out words
  d-o-g = dog

- [ ] use a Period .

- [ ] Draw a
  picture

Name: ___________________   Date: ___________

Today is: Monday | Tuesday | Wednesday
Thursday | Friday

Name: _______________________ Date: _______________

Today is: [Monday] [Tuesday] [Wednesday]
[Thursday] [Friday]

Direction: Read the words and make a sentence.

can	**man**	**pan**	**van**
một lon	đàn ông	chảo	xe tải

Draw a Picture

I Can...

- ☐ use a Capital Letter
  The cat is big.

- ☐ use spaces

- ☐ sound out words
  d-o-g = dog

- ☐ use a Period .

- ☐ Draw a picture

Name: _______________________ Date: _______________

Today is: Monday Tuesday Wednesday Thursday Friday

Name: _________________ Date: _________

Today is: | Monday | Tuesday | Wednesday |
| Thursday | Friday |

Direction: Read the words and make a sentence.

| cut | gut | hut | nut |
| cắt | ruột | túp lều | hạt |

Name

Draw a Picture

I Can...

- [ ] use a Capital Letter
  <u>T</u>he cat is big.

- [ ] use spaces

- [ ] sound out words
  d-o-g = dog

- [ ] use a Period .

- [ ] Draw a picture

Name: _______________   Date: _______________

Today is: Monday | Tuesday | Wednesday
          Thursday | Friday

Name: _______________________ Date: _______________

Today is: Monday Tuesday Wednesday
           Thursday Friday

Direction: Read the words and make a sentence.

fat	cat	hat	mat
mập	con mèo	mũ	chiếu

Name _______________________

<table>
<tr><td>Draw a Picture</td><td>I Can...</td></tr>
</table>

Draw a Picture

I Can...

- ☐ use a Capital Letter
  The cat is big.

- ☐ use spaces

- ☐ sound out words
  d-o-g = dog

- ☐ use a Period .

- ☐ Draw a picture

Name: _______________   Date: _______________

Today is: Monday   Tuesday   Wednesday

Thursday   Friday

Today is: Monday Tuesday Wednesday Thursday Friday

Direction: Read the words and make a sentence.

cab	lab	tab	crab
taxi	phòng thí nghiệm	chuyển hướng	cua

Name _______________

<table>
<tr><td>

Draw a Picture

</td><td>

I Can...

☐ use a Capital Letter
<u>T</u>he cat is big.

☐ use spaces

☐ sound out words
d-o-g = dog

☐ use a Period .

☐ Draw a picture

</td></tr>
</table>

Name: ___________________   Date: ___________

Today is: Monday   Tuesday   Wednesday

Thursday   Friday

Name: _______________ Date: _______________

Today is: Monday Tuesday Wednesday

Thursday Friday

Direction: Read the words and make a sentence.

ham	jam	ram	clam
giăm bông	mứt	cừu	vỏ

Name

Draw a Picture

I Can...

- [ ] use a Capital Letter
  <u>T</u>he cat is big.

- [ ] use spaces

- [ ] sound out words
  d-o-g = dog

- [ ] use a Period .

- [ ] Draw a picture

Name: _______________   Date: _______________

Today is: Monday Tuesday Wednesday
Thursday Friday

Name: _________________________ Date: _______________

Today is: Monday   Tuesday   Wednesday

Thursday   Friday

Direction: Read the words and make a sentence.

bed	led	red	wed
giường	hàng đầu	màu đỏ	lễ cưới

Name

Draw a Picture

I Can...

☐ use a Capital Letter
The cat is big.

☐ use spaces

☐ sound out words
d-o-g = dog

☐ use a Period .

☐ Draw a picture

Name: ___________________   Date: ___________________

Today is: Monday   Tuesday   Wednesday
           Thursday   Friday

Name: _______________ Date: _______________

Today is: Monday Tuesday Wednesday Thursday Friday

Direction: Read the words and make a sentence.

bad
xấu

dad
cha

mad
điên

sad
buồn

Name

Draw a Picture

I Can...

- [ ] use a Capital Letter
  The cat is big.

- [ ] use spaces

- [ ] sound out words
  d-o-g = dog

- [ ] use a Period .

- [ ] Draw a
  picture

Name: _______________   Date: _______________

Today is: Monday Tuesday Wednesday Thursday Friday

Name: _________________________ Date: _______________

Today is: [Monday] [Tuesday] [Wednesday]
[Thursday] [Friday]

Direction: Read the words and make a sentence.

den	hen	pen	ten
từ chối	gà mái	chuồng ngựa	mười

Name

Draw a Picture

I Can...

[ ] use a Capital Letter
The cat is big.

[ ] use spaces

[ ] sound out words
d-o-g = dog

[ ] use a Period .

[ ] Draw a
picture

Name: ______________   Date: ______________

Today is:

| Monday | Tuesday | Wednesday |

| Thursday | Friday |

Name: _______________________ Date: _______________

Today is: Monday Tuesday Wednesday
          Thursday Friday

Direction: Read the words and make a sentence.

gum	mum	sum	drum
kẹo dẻo	mẹ	tổng	trống

Name ___________________________

<table>
<tr><td>Draw a Picture</td><td>I Can...</td></tr>
</table>

Draw a Picture

I Can...

☐ use a Capital Letter
The cat is big.

☐ use spaces

☐ sound out words
d-o-g = dog

☐ use a Period .

☐ Draw a
picture

Name: _______________________ Date: _______________

Today is: Monday Tuesday Wednesday Thursday Friday

Name: _________________________ Date: _______________

Today is: [Monday] [Tuesday] [Wednesday]
[Thursday] [Friday]

Direction: Read the words and make a sentence.

bid	hid	kid	lid
đấu thầu	ẩn giấu	đứa trẻ	nắp

Name

Draw a Picture

I Can...

- [ ] use a Capital Letter
  The cat is big.

- [ ] use spaces

- [ ] sound out words
  d-o-g = dog

- [ ] use a Period .

- [ ] Draw a picture

Name: _______________   Date: _______________

Today is: Monday   Tuesday   Wednesday
           Thursday   Friday

Name: _________________ Date: _________________

Today is: | Monday | Tuesday | Wednesday |
| Thursday | Friday |

Direction: Read the words and make a sentence.

| **big** | **dig** | **pig** | **wig** |
| lớn | đào | con lợn | tóc giả |

Draw a Picture

I Can...

☐ use a Capital Letter
The cat is big.

☐ use spaces

☐ sound out words
d-o-g = dog

☐ use a Period .

☐ Draw a
picture

Name: _______________ Date: _______________

Today is: Monday Tuesday Wednesday Thursday Friday

Name: ______________________   Date: __________________

Today is: | Monday | Tuesday | Wednesday |
           | Thursday | Friday |

Direction: Read the words and make a sentence.

bin	fin	pin	win
một cái thùng	vây	ghim	thắng lợi

Name ____________________

<table>
<tr><td>

Draw a Picture

</td><td>

I Can...

☐ use a Capital Letter
<u> </u>The cat is big.

☐ use spaces

☐ sound out words
 d-o-g = dog

☐ use a Period .

☐ Draw a
 picture

</td></tr>
</table>

Name: _______________ Date: _______________

Today is: Monday Tuesday Wednesday Thursday Friday

Name: _________________________ Date: _________________________

Today is: [Monday] [Tuesday] [Wednesday]
           [Thursday] [Friday]

Direction: Read the words and make a sentence.

| **hip** | **lip** | **nip** | **sip** |
| hông | đôi môi | núm vú | uống |

Name

Draw a Picture

I Can...

☐ use a Capital Letter
The cat is big.

☐ use spaces

☐ sound out words
d-o-g = dog

☐ use a Period .

☐ Draw a picture

Name: _______________ Date: _______________

Today is: Monday Tuesday Wednesday Thursday Friday

fit	hit	kit	sit
phù hợp	đánh	bộ dụng cụ	ngồi

Name _______________

<table>
<tr><td>Draw a Picture</td><td>I Can...</td></tr>
</table>

Draw a Picture

I Can...

☐ use a Capital Letter
The cat is big.

☐ use spaces

☐ sound out words
d-o-g = dog

☐ use a Period .

☐ Draw a picture

Name: _______________   Date: _______________

Today is: Monday Tuesday Wednesday Thursday Friday

Name: _______________ Date: _______________

Today is: | Monday | Tuesday | Wednesday |
| Thursday | Friday |

Direction: Read the words and make a sentence.

cob	**job**	**rob**	**sob**
ngô	việc làm	lấy trộm	khóc

Name

Draw a Picture

I Can...

- [ ] use a Capital Letter
  The cat is big.

- [ ] use spaces

- [ ] sound out words
  d-o-g = dog

- [ ] use a Period .

- [ ] Draw a picture

Name: _______________ Date: _______________

Today is: Monday Tuesday Wednesday
          Thursday Friday

Name: _______________________ Date: _______________

Today is: Monday | Tuesday | Wednesday
Thursday | Friday

Direction: Read the words and make a sentence.

dog	hog	jog	log
chó	lấy quá phần	chạy bộ	gỗ

Name

Draw a Picture

I Can...

- [ ] use a Capital Letter
  The cat is big.

- [ ] use spaces

- [ ] sound out words
  d-o-g = dog

- [ ] use a Period .

- [ ] Draw a picture

Name: _______________   Date: _______________

Today is: Monday Tuesday Wednesday Thursday Friday

Name: ______________________ Date: ______________________

Today is: Monday Tuesday Wednesday Thursday Friday

Direction: Read the words and make a sentence.

bug	hug	jug	mug
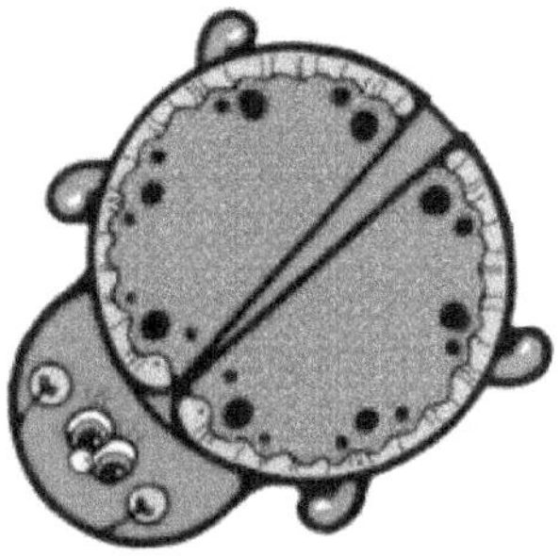			
bọ cánh cứng	ôm	cái bình	cái ca

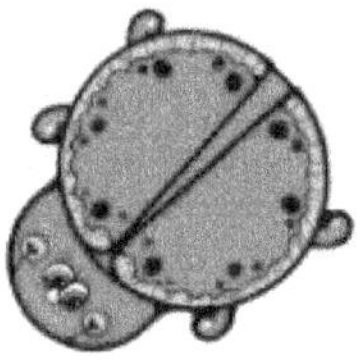

____

____

____

____

Name

Draw a Picture

I Can...

☐ use a Capital Letter
The cat is big.

☐ use spaces

☐ sound out words
d-o-g = dog

☐ use a Period .

☐ Draw a
picture

Name: _______________________   Date: _______________

Today is: Monday   Tuesday   Wednesday

Thursday   Friday

Name: ___________________ Date: _______

Today is: Monday   Tuesday   Wednesday
          Thursday   Friday

Direction: Read the words and make a sentence.

cot	dot	hot	pot
giường	dấu chấm	nóng bức	nồi

Name ___________________________

<table>
<tr><td>

Draw a Picture

</td><td>

I Can...

☐ use a Capital Letter
The cat is big.

☐ use spaces

☐ sound out words
d-o-g = dog

☐ use a Period .

☐ Draw a picture

</td></tr>
</table>

Name: _______________   Date: _______________

Today is:

www.ingramcontent.com/pod-product-compliance
Lightning Source LLC
Chambersburg PA
CBHW080842160726
47999CB00009B/2988